DISCOVERING DAIRY FOOD

written by
Angela Lucas

designed and
illustrated by
Susannah Bradley

YOUNG LIBRARY

Contents

Milk for Health 2

Dairy Cows 6

From Cow to Cup 12

Butter, Cheese, and
   Yoghurt 17

Glossary 23

Index 24

First published in 1993 by
Young Library Ltd
3 The Old Brushworks
56 Pickwick Road
Corsham, Wiltshire SN13 9BX
England

ISBN 1 85429 014 2

Printed in Hong Kong

Milk for Health

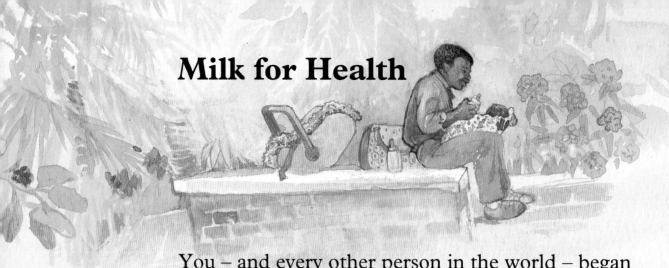

You – and every other person in the world – began life with a drink of milk! Milk is made in the bodies of female animals to feed their babies. Babies cannot do without it. If they cannot drink their mother's milk they must have it from somewhere else.

As we grow up, other foods become necessary, but most of us still use a lot of milk. We drink it. We use it in cooking. It is in the butter, cheese, and yoghurt which we eat. It doesn't

come from our mothers any more, but from other animals. In various parts of the world people drink the milk of camels, sheep, goats, yaks, buffalo, and reindeer. But most of our milk comes from cows.

Milk gives us many of the things we need to

A mother produces milk to feed her new-born baby.

**A Somali nomad
in Kenya milks her
cow into a bucket.**

make us healthy. It has calcium in it, to make our
teeth and bones strong. We get nearly all our
calcium from milk. It also has protein and vitamins
for body growth, repair, and good health.

If you look at milk which has been standing,
you can often see the darker CREAM on top. Cream
is the fat in milk which floats to the top. The
cream is removed from the top of milk which is to

4

be sold as SKIMMED milk. If it has a little cream left in it, it is called semi-skimmed milk. Some customers like to buy this milk because they want less fat, or none at all. Milk with all the cream still in it is put through a separator. This is a drum with many holes in it. It whizzes round, flinging the pale milk out and leaving the cream in the drum.

We all know that if milk is left standing too long, it goes sour. Tiny creatures called BACTERIA make this happen. They are so small that they can only be seen through a microscope. Before we buy milk, it is treated to kill most of the bacteria. This stops the milk from turning sour too quickly.

But how does the cow make her milk, and how does it get from her to us? We will find out in the next two chapters.

Guernsey

Jersey

Dairy Cows

Our milk comes from DAIRY FARMS. A dairy
farmer needs a herd of dairy cows, and grassy
meadows for them to graze on. The weather
must be mild and damp for most of the year, so
that the grass grows green and juicy.

There are several breeds of dairy cows, each
with a name and each differently marked.
Friesians are black and white. Dairy Shorthorns
are reddish-brown. Ayrshires have brown patches
on their white coats. Jerseys are light brown. As

Friesian

Friesian-Hereford cross
(you can recognise it by its white fa

Dairy Shorthorn

Australian Milking Zebu

well as looking different, all these types of cow give different kinds of milk. Jerseys give rich, creamy milk. Friesians' milk is less rich but there is more of it. Whatever the breed, all cows eat plenty of grass.

In mild weather the herd lives out in the fields, eating the grass. The farmer cuts fresh grass from other fields and stores it in a SILO. There it gradually turns into sweet-tasting SILAGE. He also dries some of the ripe grass, to make hay. Silage and hay will help to

Ayrshire

North American Holstein

In winter the grass does not grow. These Holsteins in Ontario are given fodder in an automatic feeder.

feed the cows in winter when the grass cannot grow.

In the autumn the farmer ploughs his worn-out fields and sows new seed. While it is growing he spreads fertiliser and manure on it. Next spring a new crop of grass will grow.

In countries where the weather is mild, herds can stay out of doors all year round. In other places, where the weather turns very cold, the farmer brings his cows into the shelter of a covered yard. There he feeds them on hay and

silage. He also gives them roots such as swedes, and some extra food in pellet form.

Cows always seem to be eating. Out at pasture a cow eats over 80 kilograms of grass a day. That is about fifty times as much as you eat. Unlike us, with only one stomach, she has four to help her digest it.

Have you ever watched a cow sitting and chewing for ages, as if she had chewing gum! This is called 'chewing the cud'. First she crops

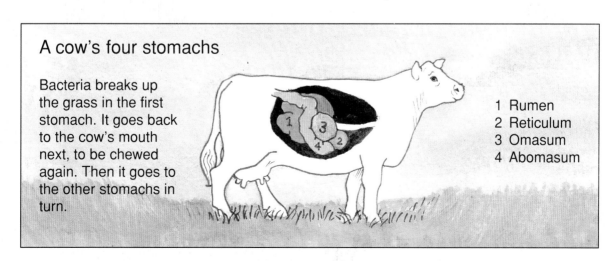

A cow's four stomachs

Bacteria breaks up the grass in the first stomach. It goes back to the cow's mouth next, to be chewed again. Then it goes to the other stomachs in turn.

1 Rumen
2 Reticulum
3 Omasum
4 Abomasum

fresh grass which she swallows. Then she brings
some back into her mouth, and chews it well before
she swallows it again. Grass is hard to digest
(you couldn't do it!). It needs all this chewing,
and passing from one stomach to another.

For the first two to three years of her life
a young cow eats, drinks, and grows strong, but
does not make milk. During this time she is
called a HEIFER. Then she has her first calf, and
her UDDER makes milk. Her calf feeds by sucking
the milk out through her TEATS.

After a few days the farmer takes the calf
away from its mother and teaches it to drink from
a bucket. The bucket contains milk made from
dried milk powder mixed with water.

The cow goes on producing milk for another

ten months, but now it is taken by the farmer, not by the calf.

A year after the first calf the cow will have another. For the last two months of that time she rests, and does not make milk. Then her calf is born, and she makes milk again.

A mixed herd grazes on a New Zealand farm. In the background is Mt Egmont.

From Cow to Cup

Every morning the farmer and his cowmen bring the herd into the milking parlour. All night the cows have been making milk. Now their udders feel heavy, so they like to be milked. The cows decide for themselves in which order they go in, and keep to the same order every day. Each cow knows her own stall and goes straight to it. She will refuse to go into any other stall.

The cowman cleans the cow's udder. Then he puts on the milking machine. It is a cluster of four metal cups lined with rubber, a cup for each

teat. The cups gently squeeze, then suck, like the calf did, drawing out her milk.

The milk flows through a rubber pipe into a glass jar. The jar is marked to show how many litres she gives. Then it is pumped along another pipe to the farm's refrigerated storage yat.

While the cowmen thoroughly clean the

This is an older type of milking parlour than the one shown on the opposite page. When milking is finished, the cowman cleans the equipment and hangs it up.

pasture

milking

tanker

machinery and the parlour, the herd goes back to peaceful grazing. Later in the day the cows' udders are full again, so they are milked a second time.

A milk tanker comes to the farm every day to collect the milk. It visits several other farms, until the tank is full. Then it is driven to the DAIRY. All this time the milk has been kept at a very low temperature so that it stays fresh.

In the dairy the milk is made ready. Most of us buy milk which is pasteurized. This means it has been heated, then quickly cooled, to kill the bacteria in it. The cream is taken off the milk which is to be sold as skimmed. Some milk is heated to a very high temperature for one second, then cooled quickly and sealed.

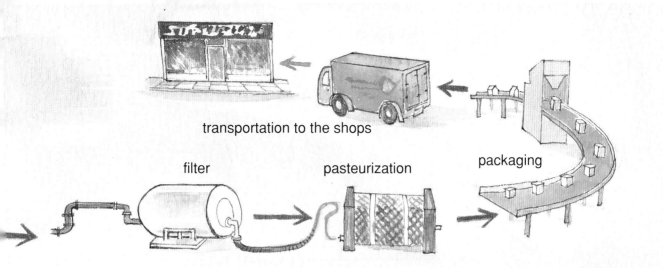

transportation to the shops

filter

pasteurization

packaging

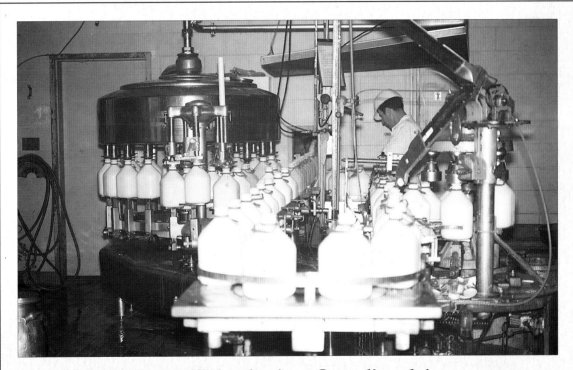

**A plastic jug milk loader in a Canadian dairy.
Empty jugs arrive at the filling machine on the left.
The bottles are filled in a few seconds, then travel to
the capping machine on the right.**

In most countries milk is sold in cartons, from shops and dispensing machines. In Britain and New Zealand much of it is sold in bottles. The one-pint bottles are sent noisily along a moving belt. 800 a minute are filled as they pass under a huge drum of milk. They are sealed immediately with a foil cap. Each kind of milk has its own cap colour, so that it is easy to tell which sort of milk is inside.

How much milk does a cow produce? At its best, a cow would give about 250 litres in a week. This is enough to fill 28 buckets of average size.

Butter, Cheese, and Yoghurt

If you want to make butter, just shake up (for quite a long time!) some creamy milk in a bottle. You will see grains of fat gathering together in buttery blobs. This shaking movement is called churning, because in the olden days dairymaids did it in a wooden machine called a churn.

Today butter is made in a place called a creamery. The milk and cream are separated (as described on page 5), and the cream is put into a machine called a continuous butter maker.

Inside the large cream separator is a drum with small holes in it. The drum whirls round, flinging out milk through the holes and leaving the cream inside.

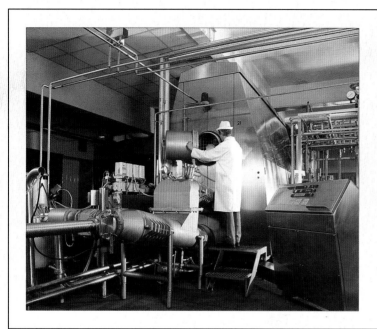

This machine turns cream into butter by churning the cream until buttermilk drains off. A diagram of the buttermaker is at the foot of this page.

The cream goes in at one end. It is churned until liquid (called BUTTERMILK) drains off. The butter which remains is salted and washed. It comes out of the other end of the butter maker in big slabs which are cut into blocks weighing 250

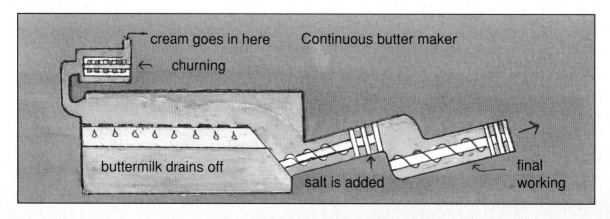

cream goes in here   Continuous butter maker

churning

buttermilk drains off

salt is added

final working

or 500 grams. Another machine wraps them.

It takes an awful lot of milk (11 litres of it) to make one 500 gram packet of butter! But nothing is wasted – the skimmed milk and the buttermilk have other uses.

Cheese is milk minus water plus germs!

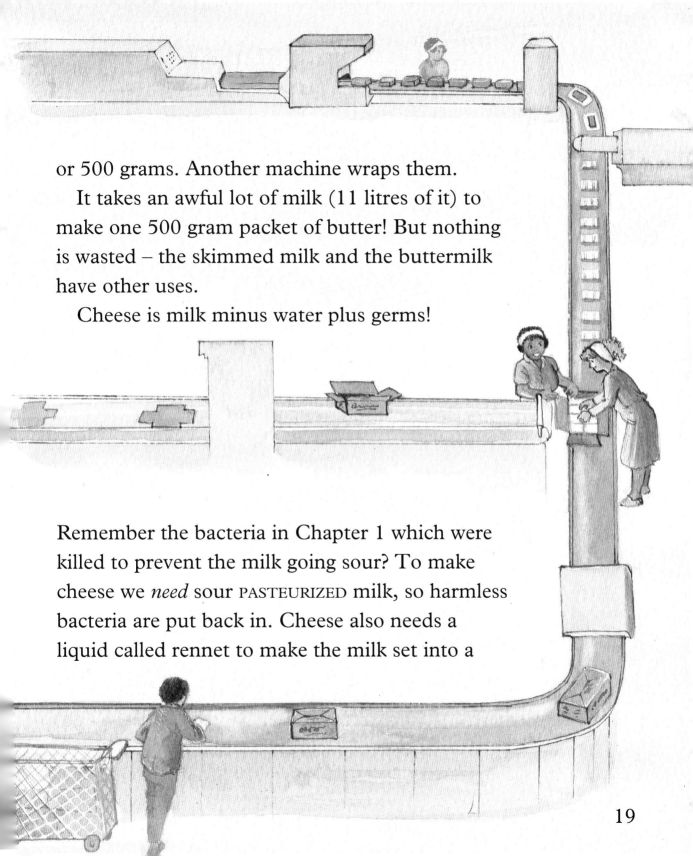

Remember the bacteria in Chapter 1 which were killed to prevent the milk going sour? To make cheese we *need* sour PASTEURIZED milk, so harmless bacteria are put back in. Cheese also needs a liquid called rennet to make the milk set into a

Stilton, England

Brick, USA

Camembert, France

Parmesan, Italy

pulpy mass of curd and whey. Whey is the watery part, curd is the more solid part. When it is cut and heated gently, the whey drains off, leaving the curd. Salt is added to the curd, then it is pressed into a block and left to ripen. After several weeks

Leicester, England

it becomes cheese.

How do you think low fat cheeses are made? By starting with skimmed milk, of course! And soft cheese? This is curd drained of whey, but not

Manchego, Spain

Jarlsberg, Norway

Anejo, Mexico

Edam, Holland

Tilsit, Germany

Neufchatel, France

Black Diamond Cheddar, Canada

This cheese shop in Uruguay has at least fifteen types of cheese for sale.

pressed or ripened. Cottage cheese is usually both low fat *and* soft.

Yoghurt, like cheese, is made from soured, pasteurised milk. Souring bacteria are added to milk which is left to stand for several hours. While it gradually thickens it is stirred to make

Philadelphia, USA

Cheddar, England

Provolone, Italy

Kanburra, Australia

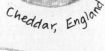

Danish Blue, Denmark

it smooth. When the yoghurt is formed, it is cooled to stop the bacteria working. Then fruit or flavouring is added, and it is sealed in pots, ready for sale.

For us to enjoy pure wholesome milk, and eat cream, yoghurt, and cheese, many people work with great care under spotless conditions. But none of this could happen without the cows, peacefully grazing in the open air.

Most milk is bought from supermarkets. It is displayed on refrigerated shelves to keep it fresh.

Glossary

bacteria: tiny creatures which live in most food, including milk. They cause milk to go sour.

buttermilk: the liquid left after milk has been made into butter.

cream: the rich, fatty part of milk, which floats to the surface.

dairy: the place where milk is made ready for drinking, and where butter, cheese, and yoghurt are made.

dairy farm: a farm on which cows are kept for milk, not for meat.

heifer: a cow which has not yet had a calf.

pasteurized milk: milk which has been treated to kill the bacteria in it.

silage: hay, clover etc which has been turned into a preserved food for animals.

silo: an air-tight trench or tower in which hay etc is mixed with chemicals and stored until it turns into silage.

skimmed milk: milk which has had the cream removed from it.

teats: nipples through which milk is sucked from a cow's udder.

udder: the part of a cow where milk is made.

Index

bacteria 5, 19, 23
breeds of cow 6–7
bottling 15, 16
Britain 16
butter 17–19
buttermilk 18, 23

calves 10–11
Canada 15
cheese 19–21
chewing the cud 9–10
churning 17
cream 4–5, 17–18, 23

dairy 14, 15, 23

farms 6–11

food for cows 6–10

heifers 10, 23

Kenya 4

milk
  amount from one
  cow   16
  from animals other
    than cows 2–3
  qualities of 3–4
  uses of 2
milking 12–14

New Zealand 11, 16

Ontario 8

pasteurization 14, 23

silage 7, 23
skimmed and semi-
  skimmed milk 5, 14,
  23

tankers 14
teats 10, 23

udders 10, 23
Uruguay 21

yoghurt 21–22

Artwork

Among the subjects illustrated are a fun run using lots of energy, pages 4/5; bringing cows to winter quarters, page 9; a Canadian dairy farm with silo, pages 10/11; a modern milking parlour, page 12; churning in the early nineteenth century, page 17; a butter packing line, page 19; real ice cream (but most ice cream has no cream in it), page 23.